ATTAINING GREATNESS BEFORE ADULTHOOD

An Early Guide for Youths and Young Adults

OLUTOYIN E. ADESOKAN

Books may be purchased by contacting the Author and Publisher at:

Email: toyinsokan.ta@gmail.com
Phone: +234 802 845 6803

Publisher in Nigeria: EL- Shofar Communications Lagos State
Publisher in Diaspora: Hadar Creations

ISBN: 978-978-584-757-4

Table of Contents

DEDICATION

To God Almighty, who never left me in the darkest hours of my journey and the Giver of all inspiration, I dedicate this book.

ACKNOWLEDGEMENTS

The reality of this book is a pool of many contributions. I acknowledge Steward Irene Ademola, who took the pain and patience to compile the teachings and arranged them.

The initial editing and proofreading were through the sacrifice of Steward Johnson Osimen, while Steward Deji and Steward Joke made available the tools to make the job easy. Mr Olumide Peters designed the cover at no cost; God will reward you greatly. Mr Gbenga Osinaike, whom I shared the vision of writing this book with, your push and encouragement is deeply appreciated. Dr Yinka Aladeshida, your input is worthy of note.

My spiritual father, Pastor Kola Aderounmu, who is standing as my adopted father after my biological father departed into glory, took time from his tight schedule to scan through the pages of this book and write the foreword. Daddy and Mummy Aderounmu, God reward you immensely.

My dear mother, Mrs Deborah Adesokan, and my treasured siblings, your support through my trials is publicly acknowledged here. President Praise, your ceaseless "Mummy, when is your book going to be ready" is preciously acknowledged, my Angel.

To all others too numerous to mention, who are part of this dream to its reality, my mentors, covenant friends, and destiny helpers, God bless you all.

To team Divine Stewards, you are the best team in the world.

ENDORSEMENTS

This is a timely collection and guide for young people who truly desire greatness. It is equally a source of deep reflection for adults and for those who want to re-invent the wheel. The devotedness of the author to the essential elements that propel one to greatness is commendable.

The brevity of the chapters and the simple narrative format makes it a compelling read. The recommendations in the book will work wonders in the life of anybody who puts them to use.

Gbenga Osinaike

Publisher, Church Times Nigeria

The right information you have and apply guarantees a life of unlimited success. The information packaged in this book is timeless, and every youth who dares to apply it can expect greatness as a lifestyle.

Favour O. Adeaga

Senior Pastor, Hope for Living Gospel Ministry

FOREWORD

I came in contact with Sister Toyin Adesokan as I fondly refer to her early in the 90's. There was a particular day when she came to me with an invitation card to a Breakfast Outreach of the Full Gospel Businessmen Fellowship, which I learnt was bought for N100. I was thrilled that a Secondary School student could afford N100 to buy a breakfast ticket for me. I gave her my word that I would attend, and I did. I never knew it was a Christian program; my focus was on the 'Breakfast". That invitation was the beginning of my salvation story.

Glad to write today that, I am a Senior Pastor in RCCG with no less than 25 years in Pastoral work. Sister Toyin is so passionate about the lives of children and young people around her that she cannot close her eyes and mind to their needs. Her long- term vision is to see the young ones around her living to fulfill destiny, even if doing this will give her pains and serious discomfort.

This passion of hers birthed a Scholarship Foundation, which she solely funded about 15 years ago to cater to the needs of indigent students in the Primary, Secondary and Tertiary Institutions at Cocoa Research Institute of Nigeria (CRIN) area of Idi Ayunre, Oluyole LGA Ibadan, Oyo State. Many students in that area benefited from this noble gesture of hers.

"Deep calleth unto deep at the noise of thy waterspouts: all thy waves and thy billows are gone over me," Ps 42:7. It takes a man with a regenerated heart, the milk of human kindness, a charitable heart, and one that had encountered God to embark on a course that will impart positively on the lives of others without considering the financial gains, even as a youth in our 30s.

Toyin owed much to God for writing this book - it is a dream come true! It is pertinent to write that, life for Toyin, is not bed of roses. She had gone through a lot; I mean a lot. A lot of pains, agonies, sorrows, deception, betrayals, disappointment, denials, lack, and frustrations. She had gone through many days without food, not for the reason of fasting, but because there was no money with which to buy. She knows where the shoe pinches. A lot of gory unbelievably experiences, too much for a person of her age.

It was of the mercy of the Lord she was not consumed with her dreams. During this storm, she discovered her purpose in life. She is a coach with practical life experiences, a mentor, a beacon of light to the teeming youths leading them to Christ to live a godly life and ultimately helping them fulfill purpose in life.

She is the Coordinator of Divine Stewards (D'stewards), comprising young men and women, raising them, and making them useful for society, their parents, churches, and immediate environment.

After six years of its existence, they have carried out several retreats, conferences and seminars, and outreaches, reaching out to different categories of Youth. This book, from the first chapter, will help the reader discover or re-discover him/herself. There are youth out there that are frustrated; so many have resulted to committing suicide and crimes.

Needless to say, that going through this book, they will discover that they were born into the world, not as an accident but with good purpose to fulfill. Finally, the God-factor in every life pursuit is clearly emphasized.

I am not only recommending this book for youths and young adults, but also for parents, foster parents, guardians, teachers, counsellors, pastors, children's teachers, and youth pastors. It will bless the life of the readers.

Pastor 'Kola Aderoumu

RCCG, Oyo Province 8, Ibadan Region 21

PREFACE

After the initial early-stage home training and socialisation during their formative age, every child acquires other diverse information or knowledge from different sources. These mostly and unlikely censored information gathered via social media, electronic media, and peer pressure have resulted in the release of youths who don't know right from wrong and live less than the age brackets' moral standard and societal expectations.

Youth will never do better until he knows better. The information supplied or available will, therefore, determine the decision any youth will make. Thus, for a child to grow into a decent and useful youth to himself and society, he must be furnished with relevant, accurate, and applicable information or knowledge that can form and produce him.

Attaining Greatness Before Adulthood is a compilation of different youth-oriented topics ladened with the right knowledge to raise youths with a balanced and purposeful lifestyle, Spirit, Soul, and body.

This book will, therefore, be of immense blessing to the youth of all denominations, races, and religions who desire to be furnished with the truth that ensures they stand out, enjoy exciting youthful years, and attain great adulthood.

Olutoyin E. Adesokan

October 2021

Chapter One

WHO ARE YOU?

Anywhere someone appears, the first question they are asked is, "who is that?" if the person is at a distance, or "who are you?" if such is close by. The journey to greatness and fulfilment begins with an understanding of who we are.

Many have been lost in life's journey because they only exist on the earth without an adequate understanding of who they are and what God created them for.

Who are you means what your identity is?

Identity is deeper than gender, which people can see. Who you are or your identity can be defined as the difference or character that marks an individual from the rest of the same kind?

The identity of a man or something is in its characteristics. Characters, feelings, or beliefs are attributes that distinguish a person or something from another. This then means no matter how identical twins may be, they are still different from each other. Everyone is peculiar and diverse in all senses. Your identity may include your name, but your identity is deeper than that.

Interestingly, there are several identities that individuals can put on. Some of them are discussed below:

1. **Individual/personal identity**: this is given to a person at an early stage in life by parents or the government.

2. **Social identity:** This is given by gender or social groups, e.g., educational, and religious or ethnic group.

3. **Collective identity:** this is given by the environment or professions a person engages in. For instance, an identity of bribery and corruption has been associated or given to some uniformed professions in Nigeria.

As a person, you may not have the power to decide the identity you get early in life, but the good news is that you don't have to die with the identity given to you by parents, social class or environment.

4.	**Situational Identity:** This comes as a result of your background or situations you are surrounded by.

Identity crisis

As we grow and approach adolescence, we have a strong desire to become somebody or have an identity, which often leads to "IDENTITY CRISIS." Once there is an identity crisis, an individual starts living a FALSE LIFE, that is, pretending to be who you are not. One of the ways to identify a person with a false life is when they borrow pose. A man with an identity crisis always wants to impress by oppressing and not expressing himself.

Moreover, at the identity crisis stage, a person becomes confused about what they want to become. You see a youth dressed as a religious person on Sunday and dressed like a model or a musician during the week. It's so unfortunate that some people struggle with this syndrome till they die.

At the identity crisis stage, so many options stare at youth in the face, which ends up confusing them. Identity crisis, most often, leads to "IDENTITY THEFT." When this is at play, a person chooses to do things, dress, speak, and/or act like someone else. They bear their personal identity but act other people's way of life.

Identity theft is using someone else's name and personal information to obtain things. It is living on another person's identity or identities. Unfortunately, identity theft or impersonation is PUNISHABLE under any country's criminal code. By implication, copying or living on another's identity is punishable by our Maker.

Identity crisis can make a man desire to become a woman (transgender syndrome). It may lead to a facial transplant or body enhancement to looking like someone else. It leads people into choosing professions and careers they are not cut out for.

Understand that who you are not created to be, you cannot be and cannot become. Identity theft cannot give fulfilment in life; it often leads to frustration because there is always a consciousness in every man or woman to be themselves.

How Can I Discover My True or Right Identity?

Discovering your identity is a journey worth embarking on if you really want to live fulfilled. At the same time, bear in mind that no matter how far you have gone in the wrong path, the day you discover your true identity becomes the day when things begin to work for the better for you. So then, how do you discover your true identity?

- Link up with your Maker

A man does not issue an identity card to himself or herself; an employer or country issues it. It thus means that you cannot give an identity to yourself. An employer or countries have their parameter by which an ID card is issued. To have a right or true identity, the first step in the process is to link up with your Maker.

- Self Awareness and Self Discovery

According to the late Myles Munroe, the greatest discovery in life is self-discovery, and

     Attaining Greatness Before Adulthood

until you find yourself, you will always be someone else. Self- discovery is a long-life journey of exploring your inner self, trying to know more about you, your potentials, and your purpose. It is a series of events whereby a person attempts to determine how they feel personally about issues and opinions rather than following the opinions of others.

It is self-examination and analysis of one's life to discover or realise one's spiritual and intellectual capacity. But then, note that self-discovery begins with self-reflection. Taking some time to reflect and think about who you are and why you do what you do is about self-reflection.

When self-reflection is well done, it leads to self-awareness. At this stage, you are beginning to know who you are. Also, to further discover yourself, self- awareness must lead to self-exploration, digging deep into your roots, the family you come from, your environments and your relationship. Do you know why? These are all that form you.

The last stage of self-discovery is self-knowledge. At this stage, you can define yourself in a sentence. You are transparent to yourself.

Unfortunately, people fear carrying out this self- discovery because they fear what they will discover about themselves, like their weaknesses, threats, and shortcomings. Nevertheless, it is better to discover your weakness and work at it than shy away or pretend as if it does not exist.

Why Self-discovery?

Until you truly discover yourself, you are bound to make wrong choices in life on all fronts - career, marriage, business partnership etc. Lack of self-discovery leads to an identity crisis.

Self-discovery leads to a life of consistency in all things, and it births finding the purpose of your existence. Don't forget that only self-discovery guarantees self-fulfilment.

'Hows' of Self Discovery

1. Look critically into yourself to determine your SWOT (Strength, Weakness, Threats, Opportunities).

2. Determine what personality type you are – Sanguine, Choleric, Melancholy, or Phlegmatic.

3. Look into yourself and list your talents, gifts, and skills.

4. Consider your motivations and fears.

   Finally, you and God are the most important factors in the journey to discovering yourself. God is your Maker. He wired, coupled, and packaged you for your existence on the earth. You can't know yourself better than Him. Talk to him to help you discover yourself. After prayers, you can then engage in self-reflection.

Chapter Two

CAPACITY BUILDING FOR MAXIMUM PRODUCTIVITY

There are lots of things that guarantee success in the journey to greatness. As a youth, wishful thinking does not achieve anything; knowing what to do and doing them well translates wishes into reality. As much as possible, one of the requisites for success is building capacity to accommodate all that God wants to have you do and effectively executing them.

The level of capacity you have built determines your level of productivity in life. Those who achieve greatness have learned to do something - build capacity. Interestingly, the more you invest in building yourself up for success, the more your chances of achieving it eventually.

Before Jesus began his earthly ministry, he ensured that he built the capacity to see him through his journey on the earth. At an early stage of his life, 12 years to be precise, the Bible tells us that he was already amongst doctors of the law listening and asking questions. Little wonder, when he started eventually, he knew what to say and how to act at every given time and situation.

What is capacity?

It is the power you have to perform a function, the maximum that something can contain. Interestingly, every wise man would always go for the best capacity. With that understanding, capacity building is a process of developing and strengthening one's skills and talents to thrive.

There are basically three realms where you must build capacity: body, soul (mind, will, and emotions), and spirit. It is essential to understand that your capacity is not what you are good at but what you can do. It is like a potential, something buried inside of you.

Setting goals is good, and much encouraged. It is a fact that a goal not set cannot be achieved. This means the importance of goal setting cannot be overemphasised. Nevertheless, you must understand that setting goals is one thing and achieving the set goals is another thing. What translates your goal to reality is the capacity to have built to make things happen.

However, a goal or goals set on faulty premises or intentions will never be achieved. Goals set based on societal pressure or pure negative and rivalry competition, and the likes will not see the light of the day. Do you know why? Strength and personality differ, so if you set your goals based on competitive reasons and lack strength and capacity, such goals will not be achieved.

How to Build Capacity

1. Determine/identify your capacity

Identifying your capacity will include adequate knowledge of your SWOT (strength, weakness, opportunities, and threats), skills, talents, and giftings. Sometimes, your gender, academic qualification, and family background will aid you in determining your capacity.

2. Identify the building blocks

Building capacity definitely include blocks that entail the following:

a. Mentoring/Coaching: It is very critical to building capacity. You must identify those who have succeeded in the area of your pursuit and align with them. Mentoring and coaching allow you to learn more about your talents, skills, and gifts. You don't get better than the knowledge you have. There is an adage that the day you stop learning, you stop growing. You will need to attend seminars, conferences etc.

b. Practice: Mentorship is also a platform to put into practice what you have learned. Remember, practice makes perfect. Good mentoring is a platform for practising your skills, talents etc. A good mentor will always allow you to practice under/ with him or her. Your strength and opportunities are consolidated while weaknesses and threats are taken care of.

c. **Financial resources:** You can't outrightly build capacity without financial commitment. As earlier mentioned, there may be a need to attend seminars and conferences, which will demand some cash. In building your capacity, consideration must be given to how much money is involved. You may need to do some legitimately strange things to raise funds to attend meetings that will help you.

d. Emotional stability, basically courage, will be needed while building your capacity. There may be disappointment or failures in the process, but you must be courageous when you fall to rise again.

3. Build with God

No man can have a rounded or complete life without God. Start with the most important, which is the spiritual aspect. God gives all gifts, skills, and abilities. So, you must carry Him along. You must contact Him from time to time through prayers and meditation to know what next to do. When you need strength to push on or lack inspiration, He is the best to call.

4. Invest time and be patient

Building requires enough time and process. How much time you have to your advantage is one of the building blocks to capacity. At the same time, you must understand that your time investment must be at the right time. This is because, at a certain age, your dream of building capacity in a particular area may end up as a mirage. A man at 45 trying to build capacity for a career in football is a joker

Hindrances to capacity building

1. *Flattery*

We live in a world where people no longer celebrate but flatter others. They hype people with raw talents and gifts, making the flattered think they are the best without considering mentoring, coaching, learning, and other things that can improve his life. Such, though with gifts, may not build capacity for maximum productivity.

2. *Early contentment of fulfilment*

Some rest on their oars too early because they won an award or excelled in a competition, not realising they can still do more. No matter how well you are doing with your skills, there is still room for improvement. You can get better and do better, but you stop capacity building when you relax and become satisfied with what you have.

3. *Overestimate yourself*

Pride sets in for some people with the little they know or do and feel there is no need to learn or partner with others. Some music stars win Grammys because of collaboration with others; they realise a partnership is better and no man is indispensable. Never think you are the best, or no other can overtake you; anything can happen.

4. *Laziness and lack of self-motivation*

Some are mentally lazy and bodily sluggish, so they miss opportunities for learning and practising. Some don't want to be stretched or stressed. At any sight of responsibility and commitment, some withdraw. A capacity can't be built without expending energy.

Boosters to Capacity Building

1. *Self-motivation*

Always learn to encourage yourself. Say affirmative words concerning yourself, skills, talents, and projects. Nobody can motivate you better than yourself. Never confess negative about yourself. Envision a beautiful future about your skills, talents, and gifts.

2.　*Set a clear goal*

Without a clear goal of the height, you want your capacity to stand, any height will look good. Write the standard and the extent to which you want your capacity developed. State what you intend your productivity level to be.

3.　*Right company*

Friendship is not by force but by choice. Like minds encourage each other to travel far. Choose a friend that has vision and is of a high standard. Friends who are mediocre won't allow you to stretch nor polish your talents, giftings, and skills. A lazy friend will infest you with laziness. Travel with those that are going where you are envisaging and even farther.

4.　*Build your life*

All-round capacity building, not just in career or profession, is essential. Build your emotional life and spiritual life. Build your mental capacity, social capital (Strategic relationships), and other vital areas of your life.

Chapter Three

YOUTH IN PURSUIT (PT 1)

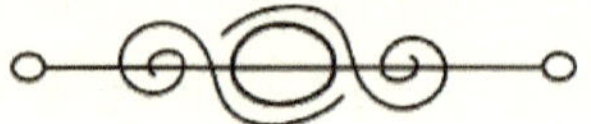

Life is in motion; it is not static. Interestingly, everyone is moving in a direction even when they think they head nowhere. God didn't create you to be at a spot. A good proof of this is your growth level; the way you are now is not how you were born. You have grown, or better still, you are growing. But then, it is worth asking what you are running after.

Pursuit means an act of running after something, trailing after something with passion or high energy. Your pursuit of something is your attempt at achieving it. Someone in pursuit must either be running after something, or something is running after him. Thus, a person is being pursued, or he is pursuing something.

But then, are you to be pursued or pursue something? What are you to pursue, or what is supposed to pursue you? Life, for some, is a rat race or running in a cycle for survival, both of which are not supposed to be. Before you can attain a significant height in life, you must define what gets you out of bed in the morning and motivates you to rush out.

Unfortunately, many are motivated by several things, including job security, financial freedom, relevance, self-improvement, and property acquisition. Please note that these things are not bad in themselves. On the other hand, what is pursuing some people could be people's opinions, approval, expectations, and standards.

Some are pursuing other expectations and never anything personal. Note that if there is anything you must pursue or that must pursue you, it must be your personal dreams, vision, and purpose. This is because the discovery of purpose, fulfilment of dreams, and vision produce or birth money, fame, fulfilment. Vision and dreams give the right perspective to life, and it has a way of giving direction to your pursuits, including your education, marriage, and career.

Achieving greatness is not by daydreaming; you must take calculated steps to make things happen. To be an exceptional youth who makes a difference in his generation with maximum impact, there are vital things you must know and do. They are discussed below:

Have a goal

A goal is the object of a person's ambition or effort, an aim or a desired result. It is an idea of a person's future envisions, plans, and commits to achieve with a deadline attached. It is the breaking down of man's overall dream into smaller bits. Goals can also be said to be milestones you intentionally set for yourself with objectives and a timeline. The fact about a goal is that without a vision, dream, mission, or cause in place, there can't be goals.

Everybody is given birth to raw, not refined in any form. For a man to be matured or refined and be put to optimal use, he must be grown in the three realms of man, spirit, soul, and body. There is a process for a man to grow, and for the process to be achieved, it won't be accidental; it must be deliberate.

Setting goals is imperative for you. When you have a goal in place, it helps in decision-making, builds a disciplined life, and structures your lifestyle. Until you set goals, you can never make meaningful progress; you just move as the situation directs. Goal setting will help you measure your growth and progress and how to review them.

You need to set physical goals, including educational, career, financial, investment, marriage, relationship, and health, among others. Also, set soulish goals that will incorporate your emotional and mental issues, attitudes, thinking patterns, relationships, habits formation, reading, and responsibility to others.

Lastly, the spiritual goals that you set focus on your relationship with God. So, you must put your prayer life, religious beliefs, doctrines, choice of place of worship, and the likes into consideration.

Nevertheless, don't forget that to achieve your goals, you must pen them down, read them to yourself from time to time, and believe that what you have set is achievable. Your commitment and discipline are two important things you must inculcate.

Seek opportunities

The word opportunity can be defined as a favourable moment made for doing something or a set of circumstances that makes it favourable for doing something. Knowing that you cannot do everything at any time, it is an exploitable set of circumstances with uncertain outcomes requiring timely commitments.

Unfortunately, many people lose opportunities because they were either unprepared for it or lacked the required skills. Some are as a result of a false sense of life satisfaction. This set of people live in a comfort zone and fail to reach out for the next level.

For some other people, their problem is pride and low self-esteem. Some feel too big, too important, or unqualified to do certain things to move to the next level, yet poor perspective about life has limited some people in life. As much as there are opportunities everywhere, failure to see them in everything and

     Attaining Greatness Before Adulthood

everywhere automatically hinders a person from getting one.

You must always understand that there is no self-made man, and you need the right opportunities to meet with the right people that will connect you with fulfilment in the pursuit of your goals. Always look for opportunities to serve humanity, and always have good attitudes about your passion for seeing others progress. In so doing, you create an enabling environment for you to rise in life.

While you can think of being fruitful with what you know how to do best, you need passion to do it to benefit humanity and those around you. A youth with a pursuit looks for opportunities to improve their skills and, more importantly, impact people's lives.

Importantly, they look for opportunities to serve God better. This principle will always turn out to be the most valuable opportunity anyone can ever identify. In Him, you will find the route to every other opportunity you need to succeed in life. Richard Branson said, "If someone offers you an amazing opportunity and you are not sure you can do it, say yes, take the bold step, then quickly learn how to do it later."

Maintain a standard

A standard is a form of measurement. It is a universally accepted unit, value, model, example, or point of reference usually applied as a basis of comparison or as a norm that is obtainable throughout diverse communities worldwide. If the way you behave or act is only acceptable to you, it will be hard before you can be a point of reference. You have to attain the level of a standard youth.

As a youth with a standard, your goals and morals must be acceptable worldwide. If your reasoning is up to the expectation of only your family, then you are most likely a sub-standard youth. It is important to note your Maker (GOD).

Three key ingredients needed to either make a product up to standard or sub-standard include raw materials, preparation process, and measurement. You can never be standard if these three things are not in place. But then, it is worth asking what realm you are expected to be a standard? Three areas that you must maintain a standard include these:

1. The spirit realm. You must maintain a good connection with your Maker. He takes the first place and remains the most important personality in your life.

2. The body realm. As a unique youth, you must consider every sense organ of your body. What you do with your organs matters. You have to be disciplined because to be standard is not about your emotions or feelings alone, it's more about knowing and doing the rightful things needed at the right time and places. Your outward appearance, including your mode of dressing and what comes out of your mouth, must all show the level of standard you maintain.

3. The soulish realm. Your soulish realm is your seat of intellect. It's where you process the majority of your feelings, emotions, and decisions. That's why it's important to think before making decisions in life. Do not be a shallow person. There isn't supposed to be any competition in our thinking realm.

   To achieve this, it is good to learn or research what is acceptable in business, dressing, communication. Also, you must be disciplined because you cannot be a standard youth until you live above your feelings and emotions. Then, you have to be tenacious about the information you gather; don't just know things from your field alone, do research, use your brain. Until you are balanced in spirit, soul, and body, you cannot make a difference.

Have a mission

A mission is a duty or purpose for which a person is sent. It is that which one believes to have been chosen by God to accomplish on earth. A mission is a journey or an assignment. Every man born always has the thirst to become somebody or arrive at a destination. It is so unfortunate that some factors impede people's actualisation of this.

Factors like educational systems, including outdated syllabus, strikes, high education fees, and inconsistency of educational structures from time to time; and cultural beliefs, including people's opinions, poverty, and lack of mentoring, hinder one's actualisation's mission. Without a specific mission, a youth becomes a wanderer (vagabond) without self-worth or self-actualisation.

As a man on a mission, you must stay prepared all the time. Prepare for journey hazards, adversity, disappointment, failure and so on because they are part of the things you will likely face in your journey. A youth on a mission must be spiritually, emotionally, mentally, and physically prepared.

Besides, have and develop a road map for the journey. This is why it is important to seek to know the terrain of your destination, and as much as possible, travel light; cut off excess luggage, let go of negative habits, unnecessary relationships, and other things that might impede the success of your journey. Travel with only required and most important tools

Importantly, be involved in only selective and strategic relationships or partnerships. You should know that not everybody is going where you are going; their travelling with you may truncate your journey. So, you can see why focus is essential for you? Have your eyes continuously on the ball of your destination.

To make your mission accomplishable, you must not and never be too excited about your mission, neither must you be lazy. Also, don't procrastinate actions needed to be taken, and never follow the crowd; your mission is unique, and so, you must not follow the multitude. Don't follow others' plans; know your design. Discouragement will set in, but you will surely overcome it when you have built the capacity to withstand it. Never leave GOD out of your plan.

BE INFORMED

Information entails facts provided or learned about something or someone. It can mean knowledge that you get about someone or something, facts, or details about a subject. Information is timely data; it increases one's understanding and decreases uncertainty. Additionally, information is knowledge acquired through a study or an experience.

Information is valuable, and no one can do without it. Information can affect behaviours, decisions, or outcomes, and it can also save time and reduce stress. Information can turn the poor into wealthy; people always need information and are ready to pay whoever has it. Quality decision-making can only be achieved by the information you have.

          Attaining Greatness Before Adulthood

Information is power, and it must be sought for and gathered. Information is sectoral and must be sorted. In fact, it will interest you to know that life is information, and information is life. At the same time, understand that most of the time, information is never free.

Youth becomes informed when they have timely, specific, accurate, factual, and relevant data about life situations. A youth without adequate and right information is deformed, while a youth with information is a youth with power.

You must understand that we are in the information age, which is why you must be adequately informed about a matter to make a quality decision. The quality of information you have access to determines how much money you will make and the quality of life you will live.

The three vital areas of your life where you must seek information are physical, mental, and spiritual matters. Nevertheless, until you see the need for information, the motivation and willingness to pay the price to acquire it will not be there.

So then, how do you get information? Reading books, including autobiographies and biographies, history, research work, embarking on meaningful journeys with a quest to learn or know more, and news bulletins, are important to get information.

Also, take time to watch documentaries, attend seminars and conferences, listen to the news, participate in mentoring classes, and engage search engines with definite questions or topics you want to know more about, will help you. Then, don't forget that you are not informed until you apply the information gathered.

Chapter Four

YOUTH IN PURSUIT (PT 2) BE GRATEFUL

The generation we are in now is filled with many youths who are not grateful but unthankful and blaspheme. Interestingly, your level of gratitude determines your altitude in any organisation you get into.

To be grateful is to acknowledge or admit a person as a source of something, opportunity, impact, or recognising the importance of a source of pleasure, growth, help. It also means showing appreciation. Every grateful person is always humble; they are not afraid or threatened, and they take responsibility. They have no sense of entitlement.

There are people in your life you should be grateful to; some of them include the following:

Parents

Especially to our mother, the fact that she did not abort you should be grateful to her. At the same time, you should be grateful to your teachers. No matter who you are today, somebody trained you, and you have to be thankful. One of the ways to be thankful to your parents is to celebrate them on their birthdays.

To your spiritual fathers/mothers, you should learn to acknowledge and admit their roles in your life.

Friends

Another set of people you should be grateful to are the quality friends in your life. Be physically present at their functions when it is convenient. This is because anyone who wants to go far in life needs people; when you stand for people, you see people stand for you.

Society

Give back to your community. Do not hoard what you know. Teach people if you know how to. Also, give to the orphanage. Contribute back to your society (knowledge & experience you have).

Career

Don't see yourself working for people but learning in that organisation. Learn to appreciate people who have allowed you to use their office; they have impacted you. Look back to those you need to be grateful to, even if it is once; please appreciate them.

Remember, there is no self-made person, people, institution, and organisation; whatever you are today, someone made you.

Be motivated

As a youth, you must have been through depression, discouragement, and dejection. These are challenging periods, and we must face them. We should not deceive ourselves that the graph of life is always straight. For anything we want to do in life, we must always resolve to stay MOTIVATED.

Motivation can be in a solid form or an abstract form, but then, it's an internal energy that stimulates desire in people to be continually interested and committed to a role, a job or a purpose. When it is rightly applied, it provides the much-needed internal incentives to pursue and achieve anything.

In the same vein, a motivated youth is a youth that is positively eager when it comes to achieving a goal. At some point in life, you must have suffered depression and discouragement, and these are part of what makes a youth perplexed or demoralised. Some plans in life don't work, not because it's not according to God's plan, purpose, or will, but due to a low level of dedicated commitment or motivation to make things work well in life.

Motivation is a personal thing; it is an internal force that always inspires a deep-rooted and passionate desire to achieve a GOAL successfully. The truth is that you need the motivation to be persistent in whatever you are doing in life. There must be a burning passion inside you and a zealous drive.

Motivation makes you ignore your pain for your gains. It makes you give your best and enables a much-needed amount of strength and zeal while attracting you closer to great men of vision. When you are not motivated, you will never give your best, and any youth that's not motivated will end up average. There is something people must see around you to be able to move with you.

There are several areas where you need to be motivated, including your relationship, business, and career. To stay motivated

Write your dreams down

When you have a picture of where you are going, it generates the needed zeal to keep moving on. This is a reason why it is always encouraged to write down whatever goals or dreams you have.

When you have a dream, imagine a future, or desire to achieve certain goals and heights, writing them down helps it register in your brain, and by revisiting your notes continuously, the potent force of motivation is activated.

Be affirmative in your speeches

Tell yourself good words continually. If you have a vision and you're motivated, you will surely get to where you desire to arrive at. Look at people that can affect your life and key into them. Look for, make, and mingle with trusted friends. In the end, you will discover that you are your own greatest motivator if you apply the right mindset to your personal well- being and a committed resolve not to end up an average.

Remember that the best form of motivation so far is self-motivation, and no one does a better job at making this work than you.

Be resolute

Resolution is a strong intent or will, a vow of what you want to achieve. It's about being resolute or firm. To be a resolute youth is to be firm, unyielding, and determined about what you have set out to achieve. Little wonder someone once said that "Any man that lives by chance will always remain an ordinary person."

A resolute youth doesn't make decisions based on emotions, impulses, and sentiments. Knowledge is not about a certificate; it is what you look for yourself. Your resolution is supposed to be in three realms, which are spirit, soul, and body. For you to be a resolute youth, you have to see success. You become a determined youth when your success becomes a do-or-die thing. A resolute youth will not care about the pain.

Be prepared

Preparation is an art that precedes the act of prepared living. Early in life, our parents, and teachers, both educational and spiritual, help us to prepare for the life ahead. In the same vein, later in life, we must re-prepare for the eventualities of life.

Several happenings will take place in the course of pursuing purpose, which may want to break or discourage us from moving forward. However, once one's heart is prepared for those eventualities, it becomes easier to scale through and get to one's destination. As a youth with a course, there are different things you must prepare for:

- Be prepared for disappointments in relationships, investment, and expectations from friends.

- Be prepared for betrayal. People you least expect may backstab you and sell you off or out. This can be more painful than disappointment.

- Be prepared for failure. There is a saying that nobody succeeds without failing. Not at all times will situations go as planned.

- Be prepared for sickness. People least expect sicknesses, but it does happen.

- Be prepared for a delay. In day-to-day travelling, there are "go-slows," traffic jams, and tragic gridlocks. So also, we have in the journey of life. It may be a delay in a marriage proposal, childbearing, or employment.

- Be prepared for rejection. It is not in all places that you will be welcomed and received. At the same time, it is not all people that will accept or like you.

Having understood all these, how do you prepare for them? You must and can prepare in three realms. In physical preparation, build solid relationships.

Build a strong relationship with three categories of people: people who can pray with and for you when eventualities of life come knocking, people who can help financially (wealthy), and people who have rich social capital (people who have connections at their becks and calls). While preparing physically, you may also need to invest in people's lives emotionally and financially to sow back when you need the same.

In the soul realm (emotional), build strong emotional values. The mind of a man harbours one thought at a time, whether negative or positive. So, think positive at all times. Develop your mind always to see the brighter side of life. It must be stated here that your ear gate determines what goes into your mind, which is why you must be careful of what you allow through it to sink into your mind. In adversity, please care less about what people say to you. Dream positive, and you will come out stronger and better.

Lastly, for your spiritual preparation, don't look for God when you are in trouble. Seek Him when things are okay with you. Develop a relationship with your Maker. He is the only one that changes time and season.

Be disciplined

Discipline is controlled behaviour or self-control. It can also be defined as enforced compliance of control, a systematic method put in place by an organisation, or a set of regulatory rules that guides one's life. Submitting oneself to societal norms and control is as well an act of discipline.

A life without control will always end in jeopardy. Being disciplined transcends doing what is right by your assessment and submission to a set of given rules by an authority. For you to be disciplined, you must be self-disciplined. Invariably, there is a place for self-discipline in being disciplined. You must be able to put yourself in check to abide by environmental or societal checks and balances. This is why discipline entails an integral part of our character and personality.

There are different types of discipline, including third party discipline, situational discipline, and self-discipline. At the same time, different areas where you must discipline yourself include the following:

- TIME. Your time is your life. Most successful CEOs are people of time.

- **PLEASURE**. In food, sex, sleep, and money, among others, we need to be disciplined.

- **SPEECH**. Conversation with words of mouth can either repair or destroy your life.

- **DRESSING**. You should be able to set your standard; be disciplined with how you dress.

          Attaining Greatness Before Adulthood

- **EMOTIONAL LIFE**. Mind what comes into our life. The secret of life is to be yourself. Be disciplined about your thinking. Remember, it's not what goes into a man that defiles him, but what comes out of the man, and in most cases, it starts with thoughts and emotions, so watch these areas.

- **WORK**. Be disciplined wherever you work; learn to be controlled by God.

In cultivating discipline, have a rule/set of rules touching different areas or aspects of your daily living. It will help if you write them. Then, practice to achieve your set rules often and keep getting better at them without looking at the books often over time.

Be given to prayers at all times. You must learn to pray without ceasing or season. Don't wait till there's a situation before you pray. Then, mind your relationships. Keep friends with discipline act. And as well be disciplined around them too.

You must never forget that a disciplined life begets a celebrated life. You must be distinguished; you must be disciplined. If you must be celebrated, you must be disciplined.

Anyone who wants to be disciplined must be willing to be under control at all times.

Above all, a godly life begets all the right attitudes and manner of discipline you can ever need to be who you are meant to be. You must never forget that God, being the only God who gives the power to make wealth and prosperity, is the beginning and the end of all things.

Be disciplined about your relationship with God. Be disciplined about your definition of God in your life. Be consciously disciplined about how you carry the presence of God within you. Then, if you must truly shine and be celebrated, fear God and keep his commandments.

Chapter Five

YOUTHS AND ADDICTION

One of the challenges many youth battle with today is in the area of addiction. It is so unfortunate that this subtle yet sometimes ignored habit has deprived so many of their God-ordained destinies. Many languish in regrets today because of what they got addicted to sometimes in their past. There are still some who are caught in this web but without a means of escape.

Addiction is when a person is suffering from a STRONG URGE too much to be controlled by him/her to ingest or take a substance (drugs) or engage in an activity (sex, gambling) that is dangerous to their wellbeing.

Addiction is when a person can do anything (steal, lie, fight, rape) to take drugs, gamble or enjoy sex.

Medically, addiction is believed to be a brain disorder characterized by compulsive engagement in rewarding stimuli, despite its adverse consequences.

The American Society of Addiction Medicine defines addiction as "a treatable, chronic medical disease involving complex interactions among brain circuits, genetics, the environment, and an individual's life experiences. People with addiction use substances or engage in behaviours that become compulsive and often continue despite harmful consequences."

And from the psychological perspective, it is a condition that results when a person ingests a substance or engages in activity that can be pleasurable, but the continuation becomes compulsive, interferes with ordinary responsibilities, and concerns such as work and relationship

As a layman, addiction is when a man says, "I can't do without this substance, (cigarettes, weed, sleeping pills, painkillers,) gambling, not having sex or watching pornography, can't stop Telenovela at the expense of studying books even when he/she is aware of their negative consequences.

It can be sorry irritating knowing that some of these people who got addicted to one thing or the other understand the effect but are still willing to continue. For instance, it is not news that smokers are liable to die young, sex brings STDs, gambling leads people to lose their money and even make them sell their properties, yet they are willing to continue. The challenge is that they have become so influenced by that activity so that stopping it becomes almost absolutely impossible.

Causes of Addiction

Different things cause addiction. However, some of the common ones include the following:

- High stress level

- Having a parent with a history of addiction

- Severe trauma or injury

- Exposure to drugs, sex, or gambling at a young age

- Mental health conditions, especially mood swings and disorders such as chronic anxiety and depression

- Adventure and unchecked curiosity

- Dysfunctional thought pattern

- Environmental influences and peer pressure

- Spiritual problems e.g., spells and enchantments

Types of addiction

There are basically two broad categories of addictions, which are:

1. Substance dependence addiction

2. Behavioural dependence addiction

Substance dependence addiction

Those who suffer from this have an intense focus on using a particular substance(s) such as alcohol, tobacco, or illicit drugs until their ability to function effectively daily is affected. As they repeatedly use the substance, certain changes begin to manifest, altering how the brain functions.

When someone suffers from substance dependence addiction, what happens is that they usually build up a tolerance to the substance, meaning until they take larger amounts of the substance, they cannot feel the effects.

Substance dependence addiction can be further broken down to:

- use of alcohol

- use of tobacco

- use of stimulants e. g coffee

- use of tranquillizer

- Use of sleeping pills and sedatives

- Use of drugs like heroin and cocaine

- Use of analgesic or pain killers and other forms of hard substance

Behavioural dependence addiction

Behavioural addictions or non-substance addictions, according to Addiction Centre, are "a set of behaviours that a person becomes dependent on and craves." Although some medical practitioners have refuted the claims that there are behavioural dependence addiction because most people engage in hundreds of different behaviours daily, a behaviour becomes an addiction when the addict still indulge in it when there is no reason to do so.

For instance, a person who is hungry needs to eat. However, a food addict may choose to eat even when not hungry and may binge eat unhealthy foods in large amounts. When a behaviour becomes impulsive and starts to contribute to developing a series of physical and mental health problems and the person is unable to stop, it is termed an addiction.

Behavioural dependence addiction can include:

- Gambling (sports betting, looting)

- Food addiction (some can't cease from taken soft drinks even with a diagnosis of diabetes)

- Games addiction (e.g. video games)

- Internet addiction

- Social media addiction (just being online)

- Shopping addiction

- Sex and love addiction

- Exercise addiction

- Location or place addiction (some people are addicted to a location)

- Fashion and trend addiction

Signs and Symptoms of Addiction

The difference between signs and symptoms is that symptoms are what the addict experiences or feels, while signs are what external parties can see. One out of the two broad categories of addiction have well spelt out signs.

Signs and symptoms of a person addicted to a substance (drugs, pills etc.)

- Dilated pupils

- Increased energy and restlessness

- Excessive confidence (you see this in area boys under the influence of weed and co)

- Rapid or rambling speeches

- Moodiness

- Insomnia

- Increased alertness

- Behavioural changes

- Sometimes financial difficulties (always demanding money from parents & friends, borrowing, selling their properties).

- Withdrawal symptoms

Signs and symptoms of Behavioural dependence addiction

The major sign is moodiness; when unable to do certain things or take certain actions (some get very angry and sad when not allowed to eat certain foods they are addicted to, watch telenovelas and so on). Other signs could include the following:

· Denial

They are quick to defend themselves and give excuses for certain actions when they are confronted.

- Obsession

They can't stop talking about some actions, and they are too preoccupied with certain activities. This is common in gambling and shopping.

- Financial difficulties

Most earnings go into unhealthy activities (betting, lotto, shopping, buying gadgets etc.).

- Secrecy

This could be for those who like pornography, masturbation, and sex. They tend to be secluded and withdraw from the public.

Treatments for Addictions

Addiction of any kind is treatable. The following treatment can be used.

- Drug treatment can be used in case of substance addiction (Drug Addiction). This is done to flush the substance out of the victims.
- Rehabilitation is another treatment. This occurs when a victim is relocated to a different environment void of the substance or activity he or she is addicted to.
- Psychological therapy is another treatment, and this involves a psychology therapist. It is basically

> COUNSELLING and includes reorienting the victim.
> - Spiritual treatment includes prayer sessions and study of the word.

You may wonder, "what has prayers got to do with addiction." Remember that part of the causes is spiritual spell and enchantment. I believe that God is able to do what drugs, rehab, or psychology therapist can't do. With Him, all things are possible.

Let me share a testimony with you. A few years back, I attended Word of Faith Bible Institute (WOFBI), where, in attendance, was a drug addict who anybody could easily recognize by his dressing and behaviour.

All glory to God, before the end of the ten days bible class, the guy's dressing and mannerism had changed. He was moved to tears when sharing his past life and his experience during at school on graduation.

     Attaining Greatness Before Adulthood

Chapter Six

OVERCOMING DEPRESSION

Depression is a mood disorder characterised by persistently low mood and a feeling of sadness and loss of interest. According to the Centers for Disease Control and Prevention (CDC), 7.6% of the people over the age of twelve have depression in any two weeks. Also, according to the World Health Organization (WHO), depression is the most common illness worldwide and the leading cause of disability.

Depression seems to be more common among women than in men. When an individual is depressed, symptoms that might show up include lack of joy and reduced interest in what used to bring a person happiness. Life events such as bereavement produce mood changes that can usually be distinguished from the features of depression.

The causes of depression are not fully understood but are likely to be complex combinations of genetics, biological, environmental, and psychological factors.

TEST FOR DEPRESSION

Consultation with a doctor or a mental health specialist to rule out different causes of depression is important. There may be a physical examination to check for physical causes and co-existing conditions. Some questionnaires help doctors to assess the severity of the condition.

The Hamilton depression rating scale, for example, has twenty-one questions with resulting scores describing the severity of depression. The Hamilton scale is one of the most widely used assessment instruments in the world for clinicians rating depression.

Signs and symptoms

- Depressed mood

- Reduced interest or pleasure in activities previously enjoyed

- Loss of sexual desire

- Unintentional weight loss (without dieting) or low appetite

- Insomnia (difficulty sleeping) or hypersomnia (excessive sleeping)

- Psychomotor agitation, for example, restlessness, pacing up and down

- Fatigue or loss of energy

- Impaired ability to think, concentrate, or make decisions

- Recurrent thoughts of death, suicide, or suicide attempts.

Depression arises as a result of a complex combination of factors or multi-factorial causes that include:

- Genetic

- Biological - such as changes in neurotransmitter levels

- Environmental

- Psychosocial factor

Depression is an emotional sickness, a disease of the mind. When not treated, it may and can lead to suicide.

Unfulfilled dreams and depression

Another factor responsible for more depression and suicide occurrences in recent times is unfulfilled dreams. Motivational speakers keep advising and shouting that everyone should have a dream and set long-term and short-term goals. They note that a man without a vision is dead and so on, which are not bad, except that the negative effects of those things on people can be disastrous.

Man has never been so aggressively pushed for success and achievements like these seasons; social media, being one of the tools that makes one feel they are not doing enough about their lives.

Truly, every man must have a goal and mission in life, and remember every goal comes with a timeline. However, if you set a goal and it is not happening as expected, it should not be the reason for depression.

To everything and everyone created by God is a time and season for manifestation. That your dreams and goals about life are yet to be fulfilled does not mean they will not be fulfilled. Keep dreaming and keep pursuing. When there is life, there is hope. You might have dreamt of being a doctor at 27, and now at 28, you are not even a graduate of any discipline. Though not good news, when there is life, there is hope.

You may feel bad because all your friends have left you and you seem stagnated. Remember that you were not born the same hour, same time, nor the same second. We came differently at a different time; wait for your time. God is not wicked; keep dreaming, hoping, and working. Don't allow people who did not create you or send you here on the earth to push you into depression and suicide by asking you, "when," and comparing you with others.

Your time and season for the fulfilment of your dreams are here. Depression and suicide are not options.

Rejection, depression, and suicide

May I say that it will be a fallacy of generalisation to assume that only poverty or a bad economic situation makes people fall into depression. Factors responsible for depression are many and are not the same with everyone in depression. For some, it is guilt; some are disappointed, while some are rejected. Until we can highlight or identify the causes of depression, we may not be able to proffer the relevant counsel.

Let me make it clear and state a fact of life: you will not be accepted by all. Some will reject your personality. For some, your dreams and visions may be because of a lack of understanding or myopic thinking.

Some parents reject their unborn children right from conception. If not, why deliberate abortion. If they do not succeed, they continue after the birth of the child. If a parent can reject his or her biological child, why are you depressed that friends and other reject you? Man may reject you; please don't reject yourself. The first acceptance of your person, dream, and vision should come from you. Not all men will approve of you, no matter what you do.

Rejection is hard because everyone wants to be loved. But I am strongly convinced that everyone cannot reject you; look out for the few that accept and approve you, whether male or female, blood or not blood related. Work on yourself and dreams, and shortly, your success will force them to accept you. Are you in a state of rejection? God, your Creator, loves you, and with Him, you can do all things.

For those who reject people because they have "seen into the future" that the person will not amount to anything in life, the stone that the builder rejects can yet become the chief cornerstone. They are not God, and they don't have the audacity to condemn or reject anybody for any reason.

Before you condemn the depressed and those who have committed suicide, ask yourself if you are not the reason for these situations.

Disappointment, depression, and suicide

Disappointments are part of the experiences of life. Men will always disappoint you because every man is limited in resources. The only one that does not disappoint is God. Anybody can disappoint, whether deliberately or not deliberately, your partner, government, employers, friends, siblings, men, and women of God, and so on. You were disappointed because your expectation was too high, and you trusted the wrong person. The fact that you were disappointed should not be the reason to fall into depression and commit suicide.

Disappointment is like an insult; why don't you dust off the insult and brace up to produce results. The best revenge for insult is result. My friend, it is doable; go ahead, and with God on your side, the sky is the limit.

On the other hand, please don't promise what you can't do. Don't raise people's hope unnecessarily; you may be punished by God for fake promises. Why raise hope and deliberately crash people's expectations? Nobody will kill you if you come out to say categorically that you are not capable of what they are asking for.

You are not God. If you can't, He will.

Guilt, depression, and suicide

Guilt is another vital reason why people fall into depression and commit suicide. Are you deep in guilt? Are you deep in self-pity and condemnation because of your misdeeds, or have you committed an unpardonable offence? Are you to be blamed for another person's predicaments?

Everyone, at one time or the other, had erred. We have made mistakes, committed sins and go against morals. We have made wrong choices and wasted sometimes. You are not the only one who is an offender, which is why you need to forgive yourself, accept people's and God's forgiveness. Make right what you can and if not, move on. That you are bad today does not mean you cannot be the best tomorrow. Guilt is dangerous; remove its hook from your neck and move on.

There is a group of people who see themselves as righteous ones. Learning to take things easy with people when they err is important. Some judgements and comments you pass on an offender can send them to an early grave even if God wants to forgive them.

We can liken these suicide and depression spirits ravaging the land to be "Goliath" threatening Israel. This spirit is a monster spirit; nevertheless, with five stones, David brought him down.

Five stones for overcoming depression and suicide

What are the five stones needed urgently now?

1.   *Strategic and consistent prayers*

We must decree to destroy the demon and spirit behind depression and suicide. Prayer is needed to break the grip of depression and suicide off the necks of this generation. Of a truth, there are psychological and emotional angles to this epidemic, but may I also say that "evil spirits" also take advantage of man's emotional state due to prevalent situations to lure people into suicide.

Don't be deceived; there is nothing like being too spiritual. When the devil wants to start playing pranks with our hearts, he makes us feel we are too spiritual. When the devil wants our commitments, standards, and dedication to God reduced, he starts suggesting to us that we are too spiritual.

2.   *Deep worship and praise*

Depression and suicide reside in sorrow, but by prophetic praise, joy can be brought back to the land, and depression subdued and sent back to the pit of hell. The ministry of the Psalmist is needed urgently across the length and breadth of the nation to declare prophetic praise and worship sessions that rain down joy and dislodge sorrow.

3. *Accuracy in teaching of total Gospel*

The deviation from teaching sound doctrine affects what people are looking up to God for, and when they don't see, they sink into depression. People have engaged all the five principles of prosperity and ten steps to breakthrough, and nothing seems to be happening. Why won't they sink into depression?

Where are teachings on sanctification, kingdom service, genuine repentance, soul-winning, dedication, contentment, godliness, and others?

4. *Spiritual counselling*

Most pastors are now psychological counsellors. They counsel by situations and body language and don't ask for the help of the Holy Spirit. We need to go back to the days when the Holy Spirit reveals to men of God unseen factors behind people's issues and give them divine directions. When this is in place, whatever counsel people are given and are adhered to will birth answers.

5.   *The fivefold ministries*

The fivefold ministries cannot be left out in this matter. At different phases of solving the problem of depression and suicide, each of the ministries is needed.

APOSTLES are to unveil and reveal to the church and nations as a whole the mysteries for these seasons, while PROPHETS declare over the land. PASTORS need to feed the sheep and give good counsel, while EVANGELISTS leave their comfort zones and go to the world. Then, TEACHERS have to provide us with the formulae and workings of the things of God. They should explain and expound to the church and the world spiritual matters and dimensions

Chapter Seven

EMOTIONAL STABILITY

Emotion is a strong feeling a man gets from whatever the brain processes from external information supplied. The brain is the central processing unit (CPU), while the heart is the storage centre, and the body is what reveals emotions. e.g., weeping through the eyes (sadness), laughter through the eyes (happiness), and so on.

There are basically five types of emotions, and they are:

- Happiness

- Sadness

- Anger

- Fear

- Disgust

Every normal human being must display these emotions in moderate proportion. A man is said to be healthy or stable when each emotion is displayed appropriately. An unstable or unhealthy emotional person is such that will be weeping for sadness at an occasion for joy and vice versa.

Emotional stability is a state when one has gotten to the point that irrespective of happenings around, he allows positive emotions to downplay negative emotions. For instance, when a man is emotionally stable, it means he has gotten to a level that, irrespective of insults from another quarter, he will not allow anger to overwhelm him to reply with abusive words, thereby starting a fight.

Emotional stability is when you convert negative emotions, such as anger, to bring out something positive. What you feel is what you attract. When you are emotionally stable, you are termed mature and wise. It allows for taking a right and appropriate decisions.

How do I attain Emotional Stability?

What you feed into your brain and mind determines your stability. Your brain and mind feed through:

- Eyes gate (what you see and read).

- Ear gate (what you hear); and

- Mouth gate (hard drugs and alcohol).

To maintain emotional stability, be deliberate, intentional, and selective about what you see, read, hear, and eat. Watch out for toxic people and toxic relationships. Also, delete negative people from your circle, and be wary of places that send negative signals to your brain. You have control over what you think about, so take control of your thought life. Increase your emotional intelligence quotient, and never expose yourself to what is harmful or emotionally damaging.

You should understand that situations will change, and people's attitudes and personalities vary. You as a person also are dynamic but attaining emotional stability is solely your responsibility.

More so, keep at the back of your mind that attaining emotional stability is not a day's journey. It is gradual; you may try and fail and rise and fall, but as you continue and are determined, you will soon be emotionally stable.

When an individual is emotionally stable and acts as such over some time, they are usually termed wise or matured. In other words, emotional instability can portray a man as either ill-mannered, uncultured, or immature. Does it then suffice that emotional stability can be attained, cultivated, and sustained?

If I may ask, "What value do life, friends, and your society attach to your being? A young man or woman may have "valuables" and still be of no value. How do I mean? What is the usefulness of the educational degrees you have acquired or the importance of wealth you are dying to have if it is not shared with the less privileged?

How do I become a man of value?

- Serve humanity with your potentials

- Share your money and materials with others

- Be a solution to a problem, at least, in your immediate environment

- Always be ready to share knowledge

- Make the life of anyone who comes near you better than he or she meets you.

That you have acquired valuables in cash or kind does not make you a man of value. Becoming a man of value includes displaying a high level of integrity and honesty at work, at home, and in society at large. Your value is your worth to fellow human beings in terms of love shared and kindness given. So, seek to be a man of value than valuables

Chapter Eight

SEX AND SEXUALITY

As a way of introduction, the information you have about any issues determines how you handle them. The issue of sexuality has been bastardised and given wrong definitions and interpretations. Sexuality must be discussed because of its grave consequence, which the public doesn't emphasise. Youths need to make an informed decision.

Sexuality means activities involving sex.

Facts about Sexuality

- God created man with sex organs;

- Human beings are sexual beings;

- No male or female does not want to experience sex;

- No youth does not have a sexual urge;

- Sex is the highest form of emotional feeling with pleasure;

- It is the highest form of the blood covenant;

- Sex is sacred;

- There are consequences if not handled properly.

Why are youth careless and handle sexuality with an "I do not care" attitude?

The primary reason is that they lack genuine information. Unfortunately, when there is misinformation, an individual is subject to malfunction. If some people know that what they do is not what they are supposed to do, you will be surprised at the rate of change that we will experience in society.

This is why, sometimes, before casting blames on people or judging them, it is important to question their motives; seek to know if they are aware of the consequences of what they do.

Another reason why some of our youth act the way they do is the starvation of love from family. Some of these people are raised in a hostile environment. They did not get to know what true parental love is. As such, when they find themselves under conditions where they are shown fake love, they fall for it without a second thought.

Unfortunately, also, some youth believe that doing so boosts their self-esteem and ego. Some even believe that it deepens commitment and cement relationship, while others think that they should not be left out since everyone is doing it. At the same time, some see sex as an adventure.

Types of sexuality

- Premarital sexuality is sex activities before marriage.

- Marital sexuality is sex activities in the confinement of marriage.

- Extra-marital sexuality is sexual activities in addition to the one you enjoy within the confines of marriage. That is why it is called "extra"

Note that both premarital and extra-marital affairs are condemned by society and God.

How to manage sexuality

The most powerful sex organ is the mind. Sexual activities start from the mind. This is aided by what you read, watch, ear, and discuss with others. This is a vital reason why you should guard your mind. Check what you think about and desist from watching pornography or television stations that feed your mind with pictures and images that make one prone to sex. Avoid anyone you had sexual relationships with because once a lover, always a lover.

Though you have done it once or experienced it, it does not mean you should continue. Have a mentor in your relationship, be accountable to someone, share your fears and experience with a trusted counsellor. It will do well if ladies and guys get closer to either of their parents for this purpose; it is the safest, secure, and sensitive thing to do. Do not engage in approaching ladies if you are not ready for marriage. Set limits and boundaries in relationships and friendships.

Consequences of sexuality if not properly handled

- Emotional breakdown if the relationship breaks down;

- Deep-seated pain that results in youth becoming loveless (believing true love does not exist);

- Health-related diseases;

- Dullness of mind. The brain is the seat of both emotion and intellect. This is why you see some men or ladies do foolish things in the name of love;

- Sex fragments the soul of a man or woman. Anytime you have sex outside marriage, you cannot remain whole;

- It makes you polluted spirit, soul, and body;

- Either of the partners can place a curse on each other if they feel cheated. Never wave this off as it is happening. Some have been cursed for life.

- Some never enjoy sex or be sexually satisfied after marriage.

Can God help in the area of sexuality?

Whatever God creates, He can control. If every youth talks to God about their challenges in the area of sexuality, He will help out.

FIRST THING FIRST BEFORE FINDING LOVE

Is it love today's youth looking for or just a crush, fling, or a sexual adventure? Looking for a life partner is not looking for love. What you do not have, you can't give.

Every person has one thing he or she does not like or hate about herself or himself. This could be body structure, nationality, weakness, nativity, parents, experience, and so on. Some are full of regrets, wishing they could change some things about themselves. Therefore, in finding love, the first thing is to identify and work on all these things you dislike to improve your self-worth.

Discover your worth and self-worth

Self-worth is the belief you have in yourself and the value you place on yourself. But then, note that self-worth is not the same as self-esteem, which results from external forces. Self-worth determines the company you keep and the way you carry yourself.

Also, understand that self-worth is not the same as pride or ego.

Self-esteem is a feeling based on performances, external factors, and comparison with others, while self-worth is not about what you are but who you are. Self-worth is not in the cost of dressing or academic qualifications; it helps you not give yourself to someone who is not worth you.

Features of youth with self-worth

Your worth is not what anyone can pay for. So, someone who understands her worth does not look for a man to buy her love with money, materials, sex, or anything.

- The person enjoys spending time with himself or herself. He/she enjoys his/her own company, and this never bores them.

- Such a person never involves in the comparison game with others.

- They do not look for approval or happiness for others.

- People who love themselves love God and others.

Remember always that people who have good self-worth attract others with good self-worth. Once you settle the issue of self-worth, you will find love.

PREREQUISITES BEFORE COMMITTING YOUR HEART

By prerequisites means what are required as initial conditions of something else indispensable. They also mean conditions to be fulfilled before other things can be done. As sweet as love is, it is far more dangerous. It is like an x-class with an AC. It is very soothing but can crash and lead to death if not handled well. It is possible to marry the first person you fall in love with if the prerequisites are in order. So, below are vital things you should consider before committing your heart.

How much of myself do I know?

Who am I by personality and temperaments, and what is my vision, family background etc?

What is my SWOT analysis? Until you know what you have, then you can know what you need.

How much do I know about love?

What is love, and what do you know about loving a man or woman? Love is deeper than appreciating the packaging or appearance of a man. It is not being pleased with the family background. Love is not blind; it is not just physical appearance. Love is accepting a man or woman with their weaknesses, and this ought to be without condition.

Make enquiries - Inquire of God and people who know better

In the generations before ours, they inquire from deities before marriages are contracted. The heart of man is desperately wicked; who can know it? The heart of man is deeper than what any man can unravel. So, ask God. Only God knows the past, present, and future of a man. Ask in prayers before delving into a relationship. Make physical enquiries about the family background and personality of the would-be selected partner.

Plan sustainability

How do you plan to sustain your relationship now and later? Learn what to do to be relevant in each other's lives.

Who is your mentor on love issues?

Who you listen to, or follow can influence many things about you. This is why you must carefully and prayerfully choose your mentor.

A final note on this is to choose character and godliness above beauty, charisma, career, dress sense, family background, and intelligence. No marriage has ever been sustained by physical appearance, complexion, or other mundane things.

Then, watch out for this negative trait in any man you are planning to settle down: inability to take correction from others. Whosoever does not take to corrections can never improve.

Chapter Nine

TIME MANAGEMENT

To be born in this age is to be ready to fight time. Many people experience challenges trying to fix up a lot within and around themselves, wishing a day could have more than the 24 hours slated by God. A lot has fallen from the singular thought that there is still time, just as a lot find themselves blaming their misfortunes on insufficient time.

Growing up as a young adult, there was not much that competed for my time as there is right now; the distractions from social media, peers, gadgets, and more have brought up increasing issues that need to be tackled keenly. Time management has posed a challenge for youngsters trying to attain greatness; the struggle matches both their personal and career life and, without addressing can become a big drag in their everyday activity.

To define time in bits of minutes, couple of hours, and number of days, weeks, months, and years would be to term it a period associated with one's existence- one's lifetime. It is also a set period designated for a given activity. And without learning the principles behind time, and its management, it would be almost impossible to accomplish all you are destined for. Time Management can therefore be defined as the process of controlling time or coordination of time.

The original currency given by the Creator for man to spend in getting things done during his existence on the earth is TIME. Applying basic physics, work is a product of force and distance, and force itself is a product of speed and time. Therefore, for any tangible amount of work to be done and pay to be received time must be spent. It is to be understood that the exchange between an employer and employee is that of time for money. Remember work cannot be calculated without time.

People work and get paid for the job they do; their expertise, time, and ability to manage it. This then forms the basis upon which employers pay their clients. Today's world allows you to work from home – remotely or from an organization's office desk, but neither of both negates the reality of time being spent on any work given. How efficiently you use your time then matters as it determines the gain you make out of life.

Facts about Time

- There are no unfamiliar facts about time. This is merely a reminder to you that;

- Everybody has 24 hours per day.

- Time cannot be controlled or hoarded but can be managed.

- An amount of time has been allotted to every man by God to perform specific duties before returning to God – one's lifetime.

- Time can be spent, wasted, or invested.

- A man's lifetime is divided into phases, in most cases, if you miss what you are supposed to do or achieve in one phase, you may not be able to achieve it again.

To manage your time efficiently, you have to watch what you do with every passing second.

Ask yourself before we proceed am I investing, spending, or wasting my time?

The definitions of these terms are often jumbled and never properly exemplified. You waste time when you engage in activities without reasonable purposes; gusting, chatting, phone calls, whatever you do that does not add value is a waste of time.

On the contrary, minutes used on ATM queue or Bus Station cannot be considered wasted but spent. You might be thinking, how about time with family and friends, on career and wellbeing, and other facets of human life? They all require time, and in this scenario, an exchange of it – just as you give your time to stay with others the same way they give theirs. But when an hour is exchanged or spent on an activity that is meant to take 15-30 minutes, it is not to be considered well spent, rather wasted. Oversleeping can be considered time-wasting.

Investing, on the other hand, brings about positive returns in you or in others financially, intellectually and in other facets. You invest time when you engage in activities that will bring in future proceeds; mental development, skill acquisition, mentorship, assignments that will favour your future ambitions. There are quite several things to invest your time in, and humanity should not be left out.

As much as you can, join in as a volunteer to work among the less privileged, and do not neglect your own emotional and spiritual wellbeing. You should not forget that the greatest portion of your lifetime must be invested in giving back to the giver of life directly and indirectly through your service to humanity.

How do I manage time?

The question of time management is not one that has not been answered; several scholars have dedicated their time in discussions and surveys on time management, giving references to results from the surveys to back their posits.

I want you to live a balanced life; as a youth who knows the worth of his time, and this can only be achieved when you can boast of being able to manage time without being caught in a loop of running deadlines. Some factors can make you lose your time, and some help you manage the time invested. I have carefully selected the words used to describe some time endangering activities used here for easy consumption:

- Setting wrong priorities;

- Getting involved in more than you can handle;

- Trying to multitask, when in reality you know you cannot;

- Procrastination, as a result of not being bound to your time;

- Not having enough rest;

- Lack of Organization, being messy;

- Multiple Distractions, usually from too much socialization, electronic devices, and less important tasks.

- To overcome these, you have to be dedicated to the activities that would spur the change you are working towards. Some of them are given below;

- Write a to-do list delegating time to each task as well as arranging them in order of how important and urgent they are, and set an alarm to follow up;

- Review your daily activities & engagements, note the ones that were productive and the ones that should be avoided and try to give yourself rest in-between;

- Organize your tasks and physical space too;

- Make your workspace distraction proof. As much as you can, turn off all distractions;

- Be accountable to someone on your goals & plans.

On a final note, keep in mind that time invested should always be greater than time spent. This is the secret to excelling greatly in life.

Chapter Ten

BECOMING A BETTER VERSION OF YOURSELF

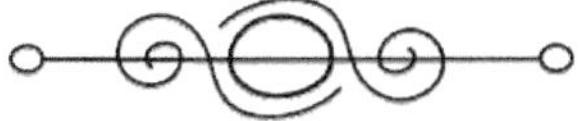

The new version of any gadget may not necessarily be better. Sometimes, newness may just be a new improved package without any better value. There is a saying that "change is the only thing that is constant." I strongly believe that "change" in this context is used for a positive connotation.

Change brings about improvement and growth. It thus means that a change without added value is not to be considered a change. As humans, as we grow from one stage to the other (from babies to toddlers, teens, adults, and old age), our bodily features change to make them more useful to others and our environment in the three realms of man.

If this is constant, there must not be a time in life to be stagnant or plateaued about who we are.

Once a new day breaks, we must become better physically, emotionally, and spiritually.

However, I will stress more on the physical and emotional aspects since these two are the visible ones that affect others. For instance, our educational, vocational, and emotional intelligence affects people directly.

Becoming a better version of yourself is the emergence of a new dimension of yourself, a part of you that people have not experienced before. It can be changes in your views, perspectives, attitudes, temperaments, values, impacts, and influence. It's when your capacity and capability are updated and upgraded that you can do more, earn more, and compete more.

How does becoming a better version of yourself start?

It can be initiated internally or deliberately and externally or non-deliberately.

1)   Internally or deliberately by self-dissatisfaction. When you become unsatisfied with yourself, you run a personal assessment

Attaining Greatness Before Adulthood

check, and you discover you can do better than what you are doing presently.

2)   Externally or non-deliberately. This happens when situations and the environment jolt us to assess ourselves.

Become a better version of yourself is essential because the world is evolving at a very geometrical rate. The needs of man are changing per second. Demand and supply for products and services are enormous, and they need someone to stand up to it. More so, market share competition and brand loyalty are so keen, and you must be offering extraordinary services or products to gain more or maintain these. Customers want more, with added value, at a cost-friendly rate.

Also, consider the fact that people are psychologically stressed and emotionally drained; therefore, this will gravitate towards a person who is emotionally stable and robust than an emotionally bankrupt individual.

Let it sink that solutions of yesterday are obsolete to today's problems and issues. Running or operating your business in post-Covid-19 as you did before then may spell doom for that business if not upgraded. The issues and problems then are not what is critical now, though they may also be necessary.

What to do to become a better version of yourself

Be current affairs conscious

Know what is happening around you, what the government is saying, what or where the economy and masses are gravitating, what is happening in the market, and most especially in your sector. Be aware of your environment.

Conduct a periodic self-assessment

Pitch yourself, your business, and your emotional state against who and what you were some time ago.

Importantly, you look inward first, compete against yourself first and foremost before pitching yourself against any competition. Remember that your vision, mission statement, niche, and others are not the same as your competitors'.

Consider your competitors' services and business operations

Deliberately consider what your competitors are doing, which are not yet, and see what you can learn and adapt.

Never joke with knowledge

Your knowledge bank must not be left unattended; you must be informed and acquire knowledge relevant to you, your dreams, and your target audience. Attend training and conferences if need be. Also, book for refresher's course.

Never excuse your weakness

Work on your attitudes. On your SWOT, strengthen your strengths, work on your weaknesses, expand your opportunities and conquer your threats.

Take mentorship seriously

Mentors have been where you are going; they see ahead and can give accurate predictions. Hook up with them from time to time.

Have the right people

Your company or those you relate with must not have hindsight alone but also very sharp foresight. Don't sit and hang around those referring you back to previous years. Choose people who talk and act while in pursuit of what lies ahead of them.

God is always new; He has never lost value and will never lose it. Everyone recognises and keeps going back to Him, no matter how they do it. The newness and better version of you or anything around you can be initiated and made possible by God. So, always relate with Him; He created your first version. He can repackage you to be better so you can add value to your world. Do not joke with God's factor.

Bear in mind that becoming a better version of you is of the most advantage to you first before the rest of the world. When you consider the fulfilment and joy attached to becoming a better version of yourself, you won't wait to be externally stimulated to become better

CONCLUSION

As a child comes of age, he is exposed to a life that he has not been prepared for. Just as his first set of baby steps were a miss until he had the support of a perambulator – which still did not change the missed steps but helped him stay upright till a need for it was no longer a priority. The same process applies to growing as a young adult.

The need for a guide becomes pertinent; one who would not mind taking you through the process of attaining greatness, even when it looks like you have erred more times than should be. And this is the purpose this book seeks to accomplish.

The world gives consent to just anything that comes up as good, but even good can be harmful sometimes. Every chapter of this book has been laced with value, the type that punctuates what is acceptable from what is good according to public belief. As you have read in this book, several factors are responsible for depression, and they differ from person to person, but one distinguishing factor is the quest to answer the call to identity – who are you?

You cannot change for the better if you have not gone through the process of knowing who you are, as well as where you are. Dr Myles Munroe once said, "The nature of something is a powerful clue to its purpose and potential." Therefore, until there is knowledge of the nature of a person, change cannot be effected. No this, and no peace; know this, and know peace.

This book offers a broad perspective on each topic discussed; to provide you with clarity, help you attain the height of your pursuit, and help you grow to overcome all that is in the way of your freedom – ultimately, building you into a better adult.

Reality comes at youths in different forms, some of which have been addressed in this book, and knowing what to do at those intervals distinguishes you from the rest. This book was not written that you would become better by reading it, but that by putting its details in perspective and making efforts in using it to build up yourself, the projected changes would surface. Hence, take the information detailed here as freshly baked cookies and munch on them as often as you can.

9 789978 584757